Poetry
from
Heart *to* Heart

Poetry
from
Heart *to* Heart

Viktor Sandalj

RESOURCE *Publications* · Eugene, Oregon

POETRY FROM HEART TO HEART

Copyright © 2022 Viktor Sandalj. All rights reserved. Except for brief quotations in critical publications or reviews, no part of this book may be reproduced in any manner without prior written permission from the publisher. Write: Permissions, Wipf and Stock Publishers, 199 W. 8th Ave., Suite 3, Eugene, OR 97401.

Resource Publications
An Imprint of Wipf and Stock Publishers
199 W. 8th Ave., Suite 3
Eugene, OR 97401

www.wipfandstock.com

PAPERBACK ISBN: 978-1-6667-4830-7
HARDCOVER ISBN: 978-1-6667-4831-4
EBOOK ISBN: 978-1-6667-4832-1

JULY 18, 2022 10:47 AM

Contents

Part 1   Dear Jelena

Jelena, My Dear...	3
Dear Jelena	4
Love's Most Beautiful Angel	5
Your Beauty's Too Great	6
A Song for the Most Wonderful Girl in the World	7
You Are the Reason for a Smile Every Day	8
Your Love Is as Sweet as It Gets	9
The World Would Be Wrong without You	10
A Warmest Smile of the Most Gentle Woman	11
You're My Spring	12
The Angel I've Met	13
You Fill My Emptiness	14
So Lonely without You	15
Can I Say to You "I Can't"?	17
Where Angel Sleeps	18
I See a Woman in the Night...	19
You Are Such a Cutie	21
Your Pure Smiling Eyes	22
You Have No Idea How Much This Heart Can Love	23
Sweeter than Honey	24
Life's Wheel	25
Night-Wish	26
I Wanna Live My Life with You!	27
May I Love You Forever?	28

Part 2   Heart Maintenance

Lightning Fast	31

Part 3   Whispers Of The Heart

Nightingale's Song	35
4-Left Clover	36
My Heart Just Wispered to Ya	37
Will I Be Someone You'd Miss	38
Call Me Tonight	39
The Game of Love	40
Hear Me Say	41

Part 4   Warm Chill

Fading Memory of a Broken Heart	45

Part 5   Final Chapter

Heart Tuner	49
You Hold the Key to My Sanity	50
Eyes in Pain	52
I Wasn't Good Enough for Your Love	54
Nothing Left to Say	56
Endless Till Eternity	58
All up in Smoke	60
Stranger are These Ways . . .	61

Part 1

Dear Jelena

JELENA, MY DEAR . . .

I wanna call you!
I wanna text you!
Oh, dear Jelena, how I miss you!

I wanna hear you voice,
Read something peaceful, lovable and nice,
I wanna hear your advice!

Thank God I have your picture,
In this time of despair,
So late . . . It isn't fair!

Can't wait till morning,
When I text, you're awake,
Your soothing words always help me out for goodness sake!

I miss you now!
I'll miss you tomorrow!
I don't ever want you to go!!!!

I pray for you,
So, you sleep well,
That you're always safe, like in a bulletproof shell!

You bring tears to my eyes,
But without any cries,
When you're with me I fly to the skies!

Too early to say I love you,
Too late not to,
I beseech, that I also mean something to you!

DEAR JELENA

Sometimes I wanna text you,
Just before I go to sleep,
But you're in a different time zone . . .
Oh, how I would like you my dreams to keep!

Sometimes I wanna hold you close,
Just for no reason at all,
Because your hug,
Saves me from every fall!

Sometimes I wanna run to you,
Even though you were just here.
Sometimes I wanna shout "Jelena!"
What?! My dear . . . ☺

Sometimes I wish you were here,
All pain would go away,
In a blink of your eyes,
It would be gone when you stay!

Sometimes I wish I can do more,
Just for you so special,
I would do everything,
And fail at nothing at all!

LOVE'S MOST BEAUTIFUL ANGEL

I see someone so beautiful so gentle,
Someone who can only be loved or not at all,
Someone with a great smile who sincerely cares,
Someone who does good and never fails!

Someone who needs to be loved like she deserves,
Someone to hold tight and keep very warm,
Someone with a face of an angel,
Who'll save me from the storm!

Someone so, so very sweet,
I didn't even know she exists!
Someone who laughs and smiles!
When she's away, is terribly missed!

Someone for whose love I'd fight,
Someone to cuddle late in the night,
Someone who shines so very bright,
Someone so perfect . . . someone so right!

YOUR BEAUTY'S TOO GREAT

Your beauty too great,
For my eyes to see,
But I won't look away,
I'll let them be . . .

Your heart so big,
For this world so harsh,
You love for most,
That have strayed afar . . .

You smile too radiant,
For anyone to stay indifferent,
You are unique,
From the crowd so different . . .

You mind too powerful,
For simple to understand,
A mind so good,
This world it can mend!

A SONG FOR THE MOST WONDERFUL GIRL IN THE WORLD

Girl, you melt my heart,
Why weren't you with me from the start?
Girl, you give me tears of joy!
Every second I spend with you I cherish and enjoy!

Girl, you are the sweetest, most loving woman I ever met,
The most beautiful cute brunette!
What I feel for you I cannot express with Earthly words,
To my heart you know all passwords!

Girl, where were you all this time,
Not knowing you was a serious crime!
The way you make me feel,
So alive, so special, so real!

Girl, I don't know how,
I managed to live without you until now!
After this song,
Without you I cannot live on!

YOU ARE THE REASON FOR A SMILE EVERY DAY

You are the reason for the morning,
You are the reason I live . . .

You are the reason I breathe,
And all the love that I give . . .

You are the reason for a smile today,
You are the reason so never go away!

You are the reason for the good in the world,
For this you should be diamonded and pearled!

You are the reason for the sun that shines,
You are the reason that my heart's in flames!

You are the reason for the good change,
You are the reasons for the stars to re-arrange!

YOUR LOVE IS AS SWEET AS IT GETS

Your gentle hand I wanna hold,
Your red lips I wanna kiss!
I've never loved a woman,
Not like this . . .

Your kind persona, I always need by my side,
I'm blinded by your beauty and heat!
You melt my heart every time,
You're so gentle and sweet!

You weren't part of my daily prayers,
Because I couldn't imagine someone so flawless as you!
Now that you are always with me,
I just know what to do!

Your beautiful eyes,
Looking straight into mine . . .
And when we connect,
The feeling is divine!

You are someone so very, very special,
And always on my mind.
Whenever you search for me,
Only love you'll find!

There is not enough time in this world,
No words could every fully express,
What I truly feel for you,
And how this love is as sweet as it gets!

THE WORLD WOULD BE WRONG WITHOUT YOU

I write this song to you,
With an open heart.
A morning would be dull,
If you don't make it start.

Every time you speak,
Every time you smile,
You extend my life,
By an extra mile!

Every time I breathe,
Every time I blink,
I wander where you are,
And what do you think?

You are so perfect,
In my special world.
Never wanna leave you,
Not even in the *underworld*!

A WARMEST SMILE OF THE MOST GENTLE WOMAN

About a woman, so nice,
I'm afraid I'm not able to describe her.
If you ever meet her,
You'll see how lucky you were!

She's able to change,
The whole known world.
Such an amazing power,
Of just a single girl!

About what I feel for her,
I just cannot say.
Time spent without her,
Is a wasted day!

YOU'RE MY SPRING

You're my spring, my summer,
For I only have you and no other!
You're all the warmth that I require,
My only desire!

You're warm on the outside and in,
Your pure heart I want to win!
I'm so serious,
This ... I really, really mean!

You're like a candle in the wind,
But the one that never burns out!
I wanna get to know your love,
And what it's all about!

THE ANGEL I'VE MET

I can see the real you,
The one with the wings!
I can see your angelic face,
The one that does marvelous things!

I can see who you really are,
But I won't tell anyone!
I'll keep the secret so beautiful,
Since to me you're such a special someone!

Keep doing what you do,
Helping this wonderful planet!
I know this is to you,
The most delightful complement!

I've never come across someone,
Like you as yet . . .
An angel like you,
I've never met!

YOU FILL MY EMPTINESS

My heart feels so empty without you,
My soul a bottomless pit . . .
Your red lips remind me of life to live,
I've grown to love you, I must admit!

Without you the days is wasted,
Time completely lost . . .
I want you in my arms,
No matter what the cost!

Your smile lights up my world,
Your warmth gives me reason to live.
Without you I'm hopeless,
I've nothing more to give . . .

With you by my side,
And your mesmerizing eyes,
I feel so loved,
As I reach the skies!

SO LONELY WITHOUT YOU

I'm sad,
I need you.
I'm mad,
I need you
I'm insane,
Only you can ease my pain . . .

I shiver,
I need you.
I quiver,
I need you.
I'm lost,
But you find me no matter what the cost!

I'm broken,
I need you.
I'm weakened,
I need you.
I'm lonely,
You're my one and only!

I'm dreaming,
I need you.
I'm screaming,
I need you.
I'm falling . . .
You're the one calling!

I'm cold,
You warm me.
I'm scared,

You hold me.
I'm out . . .
Only you I'm thinking about . . .

I'm shaking,
I need you.
I'm aching,
I need you.
I'm braking,
I need you,
You are always there—I love you!

CAN I SAY TO YOU "I CAN'T"?

I can't write you a poem today,
but don't be angry please! I'll write you another day . . .

I know you miss how I make your heart respond...
It makes you feel magical, as if I have a wand!

These few lines I jot in sorrow,
That I can't write you today, but I will tomorrow!

WHERE ANGEL SLEEPS

I wanna to call you my girl,
I wanna call you my only one!
I want to hold you close!
I want you to be my warmest sun!

I want to be the one, that you always call!
I want to catch you, long before you fall!
I want to be all that I can be!
I want you to give all your love to me!

I wanna love you with all my heart!
I wanna love you 'till death do us part!
I wanna love you the way you deserve!
I want this love to preserve!

I wanna see you, shining so bright!
I wanna know, that you're doin' alright!
I wanna know, what you dream in the night!
I want to be the one, to kiss you good-night!

I SEE A WOMAN IN THE NIGHT . . .

I see a woman in the night
With a halo on her head
She brings me new life
Raises form the dead!

I see a woman in the night,
With an emerald smile
Flowers in her hair
And a flawless style!

A sparkling like lady,
An Angel—Maybe?
She brings me dose of love
Distributed daily!

A see a brand-new love
Developing so well
Our hearts were in prison
They need to leave the cell!

I see a smile so broad
My feelings will explode
Just one night
To set things right

Your sparking eyes
Looking into mine
This feeling's the best
I know it's so divine

I see the starts in the night
I hold them in my hand
We need true love
Something so grand!

I want you in the night
So hot and bright
Hold me tight
Kiss me tonight!

You take me to the sky
And fly so high
With you I never dive low
I never wanna go!

YOU ARE SUCH A CUTIE

Song for you, it writes itself!
When I think of you, I need no help!
Rhymes come, one after the another,
I just want you, and I need no other!
It all comes along, in a perfect way!
Every song for you, bound to stay!
I hope it can match your beauty!
Because you are such a cutie!

YOUR PURE SMILING EYES

Your pure smiling eyes,
Never told me any lies.
They cry when we say goodbyes.
They're as clear as the skies!

Nothing but goodness in your soul,
That's always in control.
I only have one goal,
To love you whole!

Your pure loving heart,
Is like the universe at start.
Things fall apart,
But always stay a sweet heart.

With your gentle tender hand,
Universe you'll mend.
This goodness cannot be planned,
I just wanna hold your hand.

YOU HAVE NO IDEA HOW MUCH THIS HEART CAN LOVE

You have no idea how much this heart can love,
How patiently it can wait for it dove!

You have no idea how much it has to give,
To the person who showed me how to live!

You have no idea what it would all do for you,
Because it feels your love is true!

You have no idea what you mean to me,
When I'm with you, I am alive and free!

You have no idea how special you are,
So I keep telling you, you're the shiniest star!

SWEETER THAN HONEY

I know a girl,
Sweeter than honey!
She has no idea,
About the wonders she does to me!

She's got gentle hands,
And a beautiful smile!
I wanna see that smile every day,
Walk it down the aisle!

Her heart is so pure,
Her intensions are honest!
Whenever I hear her,
My soul is at rest!

I wanna cherish,
Every moment with her!
Before we met,
We didn't know, how unhappy we were . . .

She's a diamond,
As good as gold!
Telling her this,
Will never get old!

I can go on forever,
Saying how she makes my world sunny!
This wonderful girl,
Is sweeter than honey!

LIFE'S WHEEL

What to write,
To my special girl tonight?
When I think of her,
Everything turns out alright!

How do I tell her this?
How I feel . . .
With her in my thoughts,
Problems aren't real.

Will she smile when she read this?
Oh, I know she will!
She'll feel loved and cherished . . .
And want me more still!

I do not see why,
I should ever hide how I feel!
I would ride with her,
On this journey on life's wheel!

NIGHT-WISH

Your beauty is incomparable
You being far away—unbearable
In a kiss you save my day
Stay with me never go away
One touch is all I need
Come down on me lightning speed
When you are asleep
May angels keep . . .
You safe!

I WANNA LIVE MY LIFE WITH YOU!

I was born 33 years ago,
And the best time in my life,
I spent talking to you!
I look forward to the next day,
To hear your laugh,
And as life would have it,
Other wonderful things I live though with you!
You make me smile, you make me melt,
This . . . I never felt!
You are constantly on my mind,
Oh how happy these thoughts are,
I cry only because you are so far!
Only distance acceptable to me,
Is when you're in my heart,
And I hope life would have it be!
So nice you are to me,
The feeling is divine,
I wanna race with you to the finish line!
I still wonder if you're a woman,
Or an angel sent to save me,
And I wish this is true,
As I wanna live my life with you!
♥

MAY I LOVE YOU FOREVER?

May I love you forever?
And be blessed by your smile every God given day.
May I love you so deeply?
Because this is the only good way.
May I love you gently?
Have my heart complementary.
May I love you completely?
And very, very consistently.
May I love you sweetly?
You'll be tucked in my heart neatly.
May I love you the most?
Because if I lose your love, all else is lost!

Part 2

Heart Maintenance

LIGHTNING FAST

You came out of nowhere,
Riding really fast,
With you true love,
My heart you will blast!

You came out of,
The clear blue sky,
You came to save me,
I don't wanna die!

You arrived like,
The ace of spade,
With you I'll ride,
As this country fades!

You came like thunder,
And lighting again,
Just tell me where to go,
With you my friend!

You are welcome,
Like a miracle woman,
Come over here,
As fast as you can!

You are like,
The original sin,
When you played my heart,
I live to win!

You are the only one,
That could really save me,
With those pure eyes,
And the love you gave me!

You are so more,
Just out of this world,
Always on mind,
Such a perfect girl!

Part 3

Whispers of the Heart

NIGHTINGALE'S SONG

Nightingales make the most beautiful sound,
But nothing's worth a dime,
When you're not around!

When you're far away,
My memory's alive,
And I got for a long, long mountain drive!

The wonders you do when you're close,
I close my eyes,
And don't care what I lose!

I wish you were here,
Here right next to me,
To hold you warm,

To hold you close,
To live it is to love,
As the saying goes!

I can feel you full lips right on mine,
They always come,
At the perfect time!

I can feel your body's touch,
Making my heart pound,
Nothing can be heard,
Not even the nightingale's sound!

4-LEFT CLOVER

I wish I pick a 4-leaf clover,
Deep in the forest,
To give you special powers,
To keep you at ease when you're at unrest.

All the ones I've found
Didn't match your beauty,
They had the charm,
But wouldn't last till eternity!

To find what's right for you,
I must search for a very long time,
Coz it will save you from harm's way,
And you will never feel a crime.

What I search as a gift to you,
Is up high in the mountains where eagles dare,
Coz you only deserve the best,
I wanna show you how much I care!

Until the clover is found,
May the angels keep you safe,
Always be by your side,
Keep you away from strafe.

Just follow the light,
That follows you around,
Because in that forest,
You won't hear a sound!

MY HEART JUST WISPERED TO YA

I'm so happy that I've met you
I never wanna let you
Go on your way without me
Please give this a chance and let it be
The most wonderful love
With blessings from above
When I see your beauty, I melt
These strong feelings I've never felt
Before with anyone,
Could you be the one,
I've been searching for all these years,
To heal my heart and wipe the tears
I am so confident I have no fears,
I let you know what I feel,
In a single sentence so true, so real,
Will you let me be there for you,
As I can go on loving you,
Forever and ever as feelings grow,
I don't want to ever go,
Anywhere without you holding my hand,
Coz I cannot pretend,
That I don't like you very much,
And I'm missing your gentle touch,
Just one kiss I wanna feel,
Full of passion and so surreal,
I wanna hear you moan,
I don't want to be alone . . . Anymore!

WILL I BE SOMEONE YOU'D MISS

How do I make you mine?
Will you love me?
On another side of the world,
Will you have me?

Your beauty glows in the night, and
Your kiss—would feel so right!!
Your touch is all that I need,
If I don't have it, my heart would bleed...

Your perfect life,
Compared to mine,
I need double dose of you,
To start feelin' fine!

This love,
Will it happen in this life?
I'd fight for it,
I'd die for it . . .

I have no words to describe your beauty,
Keeping you safe would be my duty!
As night falls will you run to me?
You love me too, is that your plea?

After our first kiss,
Would I be someone that you'd miss?

CALL ME TONIGHT

Call me tonight,
Make my day,
Let me see you,
Send a wave!

Send me a kiss,
Though a virtual place,
Send me a quick one,
Than slow the pace!

Let me see your smile,
Your full lips from ear to ear,
And gently whisper,
Your feelings in my ear!

Talk to me slowly,
Don't go too fast,
I want this moment
To be the one to last!

THE GAME OF LOVE

I love this game we play,
The way I'm courting you.
You smile and send me a kiss,
You know you're wanting to!

I love when we run on the sand,
At the peak of dawn.
I'm right behind you,
Trying to catch on!

I love the late-night dinners,
By the candle light.
Your beauty glows,
As it illuminates the night!

I love the coffee you make,
Served with a kiss to wake me up.
Without the same kiss,
I cannot begin my evening nap!

I love all the time with you,
As it feels alright.
You by my side,
Is the only thing that's right!

HEAR ME SAY

If I could make it all go away . . .
All that pain . . .
If I could only wash it away,
With the morning rain!

If you could forever
Never feel bad again
If I could help you,
My dear friend.

If it could all just
Stay away
Pain destroyed completely
It's not welcome to stay.

If I could make you feel better
With just one touch
I'd gladly do it
So you'd never again feel a grudge.

If I could re-set you mind
Fill it in with good memories
For you to cherish
Only selected treasuries.

All these are just honest wises
From a good, good hearth . . .
It will all be over soon,
And you'll have a fresh start!

Part 4

Warm Chill

FADING MEMORY OF A BROKEN HEART

Every time I see her picture . . .
I stary to cry . . .
Ten years have passed . . .
And I still wonder why . . .

All I have now,
Is a broken memory,
An inflicted scar,
Burden and worry . . .

She should have been,
My only one,
But she left me,
As if I was no one.

She wasn't sorry
For what she did.
I was the one,
She did not need.

Time will heal me
Or so they say.
10 years have passed
My mind's still astray.

All she needed was,
One flight back,
And my life would be,
Back on track.

All I needed was,
Her warm smile,
But I haven't seen that
In a while...

Been held together
By a pack of pills,
When she reads this,
She'll get the chills!

Nothing left to do,
But sit and pray,
Maybe she'll come back...
One sunny day!

Part 5

Final Chapter

HEART TUNER

I'll try write you a brand-new song,
For your beauty and fire bring out the best in me after way too long!

I dunno how much longer I can go on,
Without seeing your beautiful face, oh what a wonder I've come upon!

Whenever you're not here I shake in misery,
When you touch me it's all gone – oh what a mystery!

Sometimes I wish I met you sooner,
But you cannot wish for what you do not know – meeting your heart tuner!

YOU HOLD THE KEY TO MY SANITY

I've never felt this way before,
Since I saw you all I want is more.
You shook my heart and opened its door,
You are the one who will start a war!

You are the one and all that I need,
Thunder and lightning, you are the speed.
You are a saint, the ultimate sin,
The one whose heart I want to win!

You are brighter than the morning sky,
You know all my reasons why.
When I'm with you I'll never cry,
You give me wings with which I fly!

You burn like fire into the night,
You are the one who shines so bright,
You are the one, and I know that I'm tight,
You are an angel, alright?!

You are the one, one of a kind,
You make all love completely blind.
You're the one I needed to find,
You are the one always on my mind!

You are worth every extra mile,
You are the first one on my speed dial.
You are the one who put my soul on trial,
You're all in one, and there's no denial!

You are the light shining from above,
You are the only one worth to love.
Your kisses are oh so tender,
To your love I surrender!

You are faster than the speed of light,
You are the one that shines in the night.
You are the one who will put up a fight,
You are an angel, alright?!

Without you I'm incomplete,
A lost soul with no one to meet.
Piece of the puzzle we must complete,
Another level we have to beat!
All that you touch turns into gold,
My soul is all yours, but unsold.
With you I wanna grow old,
I do love you, to say it bold!

Fully charged, so electric,
You easy my mind going hectic.
This time it's coming, so do expect it,
All for you, so respect it!

You hold the thunder, you hold the rain,
Only you can kiss away the pain.
You hold the key to my sanity,
Of a different reality!

You hold the map of the universe,
Your number is dimensionless.
You love—measureless,
Without you—hapless.

EYES IN PAIN

I once told you, you could stop the rain,
But why have you made these eyes full of pain?

You held the key to my sanity,
But you lead me to insanity!

You had the key to my happiness,
But you left me with emptiness...

After all the love I gave you with nothing in return,
My heart was stricken as it took the wrong turn!

Here comes the pain that's so different from the rest!
Here comes the pain that'll put your mind to the test!
Here comes the though piercing the brain!
Here comes the heart hanging on a chain!

Do I deserve so much pain?
You made these good eyes bloody rain.

Why was there no happy ending story?
Where is that good old glory?!

You unlocked the sorrow that takes me down below!
You unlocked the gates which bring no tomorrow!

How is it that only you I miss?
With these eyes full of pain, can I really see better than this?

Here comes the rain pouring thought my soul!
Here comes the rain that will dissolve us all!
Here is a part of a dripping heart,
Here is a man that fell apart.

Mind twisting further, on your mind is murder!
Nothing to explain, why those eyes are full of pain!

You will wish for death, when she's though with you!
You wish you never let, that mouth kiss you!

You will wish for drugs, but she's here to stay!
You will wish for death, to make it go away!

When you think it's over, when you think it's passed,
She will come again, finish you at last!

You unlocked the insanity that lives through immortality
You unlocked the reign of pain, but only you . . . could have stopped . . . the rain!
Eyes full of pain you made them bloody rain!
Eyes full of sorrow that can't see tomorrow!
Eyes that have seen what no one should see,
Eyes that weren't left the way they should be . . .

I WASN'T GOOD ENOUGH FOR YOUR LOVE

I wasn't good enough,
For your love,
You sent a death ray,
From above!

All my love,
Meant nothing to you,
You left me,
With a big fuck-you!

My whole heart,
Has burst for you,
You are no good,
That's what you do!

That fake laugh,
And a phony smile,
Haven't seen those,
In a while!

In my head,
thoughts are few,
In my heart,
A rusty screw!

You are such,
A foul disease,
Stay away,
Damn bitch please!

You're a leech
A blood suck-off,
Just someone
Can't get rid of!

You're a monster,
There's no denial,
Slowly burn,
End of trial!

NOTHING LEFT TO SAY

What did you say,
What did I ever do to you?
You deserve nothing,
But a big fuck-you!

What did you say,
You just need some time?
To think things through,
To conjure up a crime!

What did you say,
You hate all the texts?!
Just to leave you far way baby,
Would be for the best!

What did you say,
Who you really are?
A kiss-of-death,
That leaves a man scarred!

What did you say,
What do you really do?
Nothing with honor,
Just running through and through!

What did you say,
You live your life astray?!
Best thing from me,
Is to stay the far, far away!

What did you say,
You don't know who you really are?!
A cheap-fun lover,
With a mental scar!

What did you say,
That your life's a mess?!
Check-mate for ya,
Just like the game of chess!

What did you say,
You don't know what you want?!
All is forgotten, all is lost,
But I'm really, really not . . .

What did you say,
What's on your twisted mind?!
Someone like me,
Is very hard find!

What did you say,
Where did we all go wrong?
This is the end,
Just like this fucking song!

What did you say?
Shall I go and pray?
For your worthless soul,
Nothing left to say!

ENDLESS TILL ETERNITY

Take your time slow,
As long as you need.
No time to rush,
Nor increase the speed.

We shall have,
All the time in the world,
As we well know,
Space-time is twisted & turned.

We will wait now,
The endless time till eternity.
Coz that's the only thing right
And the right place to be.

You know I'll wait for you,
As long as I must.
At the end of the line,
You're the one I thrust.

I wish that you have,
All the time in the world.
For the greater good,
And the rewards so pearled!

We will both know,
When the time comes,
As we shall be
In each other's arms.

The time that we have,
We must use patiently,
Without wrong turns
Or anything unexpectedly!

All that we need
Is time till eternity,
For one kiss of life
Fulfills the destiny!!!!

ALL UP IN SMOKE

The last fantasy went up in smoke!
I tell you it ain't no joke!

When you left, so did the hope!
You made me walk the tight rope!

You said goodbye the way you could!
Left me stranded the way you would!

I couldn't even cry for help!
I couldn't even let out a yelp!

So, now I know what I loved!
Pushed away and roughly shoved!

You are a girl with a black heart!
And you played me baby way too smart!

I didn't even have a thing to say!
You already dug my own grave!

Alone and broken with nothing left to say,
I'll just sit down and pray, for a better day!

STRANGER ARE THESE WAYS . . .

Love has these strange ways,
To make you grateful for dull days.
Don't waste your time spent in a haze,
Start living—leave the endless maze.

There are way too many crazy ways,
How you can choose to spend your days.
Open the window, feel the sun's rays,
Breath in new life, start a new phase!

Express yourself, don't be afraid,
There's so much good, and no one to blame!
Since I saw you, I'll never be the same,
You deep blue eyes, dissipating the pain.

Take a risk, be brave,
Don't go through life, like going' though a rave.
It's ok now, better than before,
Take what you have, and never ask for more!

www.ingramcontent.com/pod-product-compliance
Lightning Source LLC
Chambersburg PA
CBHW061511040426
42450CB00008B/1559